Table of **Contents**

Introduction

Life itself is an exaggeration during the period of time when children leave the security of their elementary school until they have survived the first year of high school. During grades six through nine—no matter what name we give to the institutions housing them—students are forced to confront life just when they are most uncomfortable with their own bodies and minds. The physical awkwardness accompanying the onset of puberty and the unquenchable desire for peer acceptance make every day often a struggle for survival. The age group's sudden need to test the authority of parents, adults, and society's taboos only adds to the daily tension in the lives of young adolescents.

Middle school children are often obsessed and over-react to everything in life. Their blood is rushing hysterically through their circulatory systems, as if they have been mugged by their own

The Middle School Years

Love Me
When I'm Most Unlovable

Robert Ricken

National Middle School Association
Westerville, Ohio

Sue Swaim, Executive Director—Jeff Ward, Deputy Executive Director—Edward Brazee, Editor, Professional Publications—John Lounsbury, Consulting Editor, Professional Publications—April Tibbles, Director of Publications—Dawn Williams, Production Manager— Lindsay Kronmiller, Graphic Designer—Nikia Reveal, Graphic Designer—Mary Mitchell, Designer, Editorial Assistant—Marcia Meade-Hurst, Senior Publications Representative

Library of Congress Cataloging-in-Publication Data
Ricken, Robert.
    The middle school years : love me when I'm most unlovable / Robert Ricken.
        p. cm.
    ISBN 978-1-56090-207-2
    1. Middle school students—Poetry. 2. Teenagers—Poetry. I. Title.

PS3618.I373M53 2007 811'.6--dc22

2007016461

National Middle School Association
4151 Executive Parkway, Suite 300
Westerville, Ohio 43081
p: 614-895-4730   f: 614-895-4750
www.nmsa.org

ormones. Daily travails become
that seem to them to be life and
death situations.

The thoughts in this book, poems if you
choose to call them that, are emotions
expressed to me during my 30 very
rewarding years of working with this
exciting age group. The emotions are
honest; the feelings are real. These
expressions are the sincere reflections
and sentiments of young people as they
struggle toward adulthood. In some
cases these poems were written
by students.

Although we frequently are forced to
shake our heads at their antics, young
adolescents make each day a joyful
adventure. That's why middle school
teachers have happily learned to "love
them when they're most unlovable."

— R.R.

Worrying About
Moving Up to Middle **School**

I'm *looking forward* to going to the middle school. I'm excited and a little nervous.

Somehow all the kids seem to like it but they love telling horror stories about what goes on there.

My parents are the ones who are really nervous.

If they ask me once more if I'm scared, I think they'll convince me that I am!

I was such a *big shot* in elementary school.
Now I graduated and I'm going to the middle school.
I'm worried.
I don't know any of the kids from the other schools.
It's such a **big** building!
I'm *nobody* again.
I don't know if I should wish for the summer to end,
or pray for it to go on forever.

I'm *really worried* about the middle school.
I'm not a great student.
I'm a very good athlete.
But they don't have sixth grade teams.
I'm probably the only kid who both teachers and the kids won't respect.

How do you go from top of the heap to **bottom of the barrel?**
How do you go from convincing one teacher to like you
to getting along with six or eight of them?
I never before had any trouble sleeping through the night.
Now I spend a lot of time staring at the ceiling.

Those Hectic First Days

Instead of one room a day
I now have nine.
If I couldn't please one teacher, how can I *satisfy you all?*
I can't even find my room!
I'm lost!
My God, I finally found my room, and **I don't know** which seat is mine!

Something must be *wrong* **with me.**
In elementary school I loved when
my Mom came on field trips.
I liked when she was a big PTA lady.
Now that I'm in middle school I get
embarrassed if she comes near the place!

I'm sorry but I can't say I'm sorry.
I'm ***frightened*** but I'll never admit it.
I want you to like me but do things to **get you angry.**
I forget my homework even when I do it.
I break my promise to try harder.
I sometimes cheat even when I know the answers.
Don't you know that when I'm bad, I'm in the most pain?
Please don't give up on me. Everyone else has.

Dear Diary,

I can't believe I go from feeling *great* to feeling *terrible*. What's worse is that I seem to go from wonderful highs to horrible lows. This is a typical **roller coaster ride** for me each day. Unfortunately, it's usually downhill!

Why do they call art a *minor* subject when it's the *Major* joy of my life.

I used to have **dreams.**
Now I have *nightmares.*

        I used to be called cute.
        Now I'm called awkward.

I used to be confident.
Now *I'm insecure.*

        I was a big wheel in K–5.
        Now I'm a flat tire!

Ecstatic
Very Happy
Cheerful
Loving
Agreeable
Fortunate
Satisfied
Content
Queasy
Uneasy
Distrustf
Suspicious
Uncomfortable Anxious

A

Upset

oyed Argumentative

Angry

Disagreeable

Disheartened

Degraded *Hostile*

Infuriated

Dejected

Enraged

Depressed

I'm either nuts or confused.

I listed 26 separate feelings!

It's my hysterical alphabet.

Does a teenager ever have a calm day?

Reactions to Teachers

I'm a teenager—*teach.*

I go to your school.

It's not mine it's yours.

How can I be comfortable in *someone else's house.*

You force me to attend and live by your rules.

I'm frightened of you, the building, and the kids from other schools.

I show off a lot to make everyone think ***I'm not scared.***

I'm not sure of myself.

There are many **questions** about me and hardly any **answers.**

I'm not comfortable with my own body.

Help me please, *I don't know who I am.*

I'll risk being wrong when you *help me* to **understand**

I'll *try harder* when you *praise my efforts.*

I'll **withdraw** if you're *sarcastic or nasty.*

You spoke to me of *love,*
I doubted you.

You spoke to me of *caring,*
I doubted you.

You spoke to me of my *self-worth,*
I doubted you.

You came to the hospital to visit me,
I believed everything you said.

Detention again...

I didn't do my homework
I **was** talking in class.
I knocked my friend's books down.
I forgot my pen.

I wish someday you'd just ask me to stay after class.
I want so much **to talk to you.**
Don't say, why didn't you ask me?
The invitation must be yours.

They talk, talk, talk about the new curriculum!
I'd rather have the best teacher with the worst curriculum
Than a poor teacher with the best curriculum!
It's always the teacher that matters!

Why is it, *I smile* **when** *you smile,* *laugh* **when** *you laugh,* and feel threatened when you scream?

For forty minutes every day, *you're in control* **of my emotions.**

There's *trouble* in the Middle East.

The glaciers are **melting.**

There was a **tsunami** in the Far East.

A cross was **burned** on someone's lawn.

Genocide is going on in Africa.

In social studies *we just reviewed* for tomorrow's test!

When you tell us we're your bad class, **we act the part.**

When you tell us we're your good class, **we act the part.**

Is that what they mean by a *self-fulfilling prophecy?*

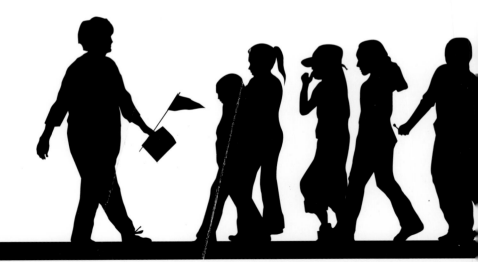

Do you see me when you look out at our faces?
Am I just part of the crowd?
Do you even know my name?

Did you notice:
  I typed my book report?
  I bought a binder for my lab work?
  I smile during your class?

I look for any sign of recognition.
A good grade is okay, but **a personal comment makes my day.**

I came to you with a problem.

You listened.
You agreed I was right.

Then you told me *not to fight* the system.
I just **began** *my search for a new hero.*

I got a B+ on my report
and was **really proud of myself.**

My best friend got an A+
but copied it from the Internet

Believe it or not he teased me
for getting a lower grade.
Does honesty count?

I have **6 great teachers.**

The *7th one is boring, nasty* and doesn't
give us back our grades or test papers.

Nothing can be done about it.
It seems she has a *disease called tenure.*

I'm in the *gifted program* and
Some people think it's an *honor.*

But every time I make a mistake,
I'm not prepared, or
do poorly on a test,
my teacher says, I thought you were
supposed to be "gifted."

I'm not too sure if it's an honor
or just another *burden to carry.*

When I was in 7th grade
my dad passed away.

My mom and I had a really
hard time for awhile.

Mr. Clark, my history teacher
came to the wake in a snow storm.

He's the only one I believe
when he says if I need anything, **he'll be there.**

As soon as I get home I check my e-mails.
Homework can wait.
My errands can wait.
Even the bathroom can wait!
First I have to see if she sent me a message.

My mother met with my team of teachers.

I no longer can get away with anything.

She said the team knows stuff about me
That even she didn't know.

I used to feel you liked me
if you did everything for me.

Now I know *you were right*
when you helped me to do it myself.

Caring is *helping someone to grow*
even if it means away from you.

Because I'm a jock
doesn't mean I'm dumb.

I like it **when the teachers
call us student athletes.**

When I'm bad
I know I'm bad.

I can't admit it in front of the class.

I want you to
love me when I'm most unlovable.

When teachers give homework on the weekend,
Sunday night becomes a school night!

The soul without imagination is what an ...servatory would be without a telescope.
—Henry Ward Beecher

A

The *best teacher helps* me to do more than answer the questions.

The *best teacher encourages* me to question the answers.

April 15

Homework:
Interview Parents

Relationships with Parents

We're **running** in the halls,

Hanging out at the malls..

I don't know what it is

I just have to be with kids.

Parents all have *one thing* in common.
They **don't like** their kid's friends!

My parents say that I don't like being with them since I'm in middle school.

Since I'm in middle school *I see my parents in a different way.*

I'm uncomfortable when they are around my friends.

I go bonkers when they listen in on my calls or read my e-mails.

And God forbid if they kiss me or try to hold my hand if I'm with my friends!

Every adult tells us not to use drugs.

Grandpa has **Zantac** before every meal.

Grandma is on **Valium** to settle her nerves.

Dad takes **Viagra.**

Mom lives on **uppers.**

One more example of

"do as I say, not as I do."

My parents are **not too cool.**

They get upset when I telephone boys.

They hate when I e-mail them.

They'd probably faint if they came to school
and saw **how I look in my best friend's clothes.**

In our advisory group a kid was
upset because his folks
were **getting divorced.**

He was going to live with his mom.

His dad was his scout master and
little league coach.

You always hear **about kids**
causing problems.

How about *parents who cause
problems for their kids!*

Latoya lives with a *guardian.*

John lives with his parents.

Mary lives with her **mom.**

Hector lives with his **grandma.**

Daron lives with his *mom and step dad.*

Marcia lives with two moms.

I think we need a *new definition* **of family.**

Rhythms of
Middle School

Parents, teachers, and counselors
always agree on one thing about me.
No matter what I do in class
they say, I'm not working up to my ability.

Thanks for telling me that when she tripped me
she was just flirting with me.

I didn't know she liked me.

It's hard to believe this sex thing is going
to get better and better.

No matter what subject is taught
these questions are universal:

Does spelling count?

Do we have to use ink?

Should we head our paper?

Is this a quiz or a test?

Does this count toward our grade?

Is this stuff going to be on the test?

When I'm on the ball field
I don't care if the whole world watches.

When I have to make a speech in class
I wish I could crawl into a hole.

I seem to be good in things that
People don't think are important.

My locker has dirty gym socks,

last week's assignments,

crumpled papers, dirty tissues,

broken pencils, apple cores,

rotten banana peels,

overdue library books,

and a lock that won't open.

My homework is on my desk.

I live with Mom this week.

And left it at Dad's house.

No one believes me!

Good Luck
Bill

GO ★
TEAM
★ GO!

✿
Cheerleader
Kelsey

I hate to go to the bathroom in school.

I like locked doors and privacy.

The nurse thinks I have a stomach problem.
since I use her john every day.

The kids in my school **volunteer**
for community service.

We help senior citizens
by shoveling their walks, buying groceries for them
and entertaining handicapped shut-ins.

That's why our school is never in the news!

The media believes, "Good news is no news."

Can they *hear what we hear?*

Can they *see what we see?*

Can they *feel what we feel?*

Pain, sorrow, happiness, and joy make up our life in middle school.

You ask, ***"Why not give it up?"***

Because there's **nothing quite like** these teenage years!

Samantha is **beautiful.**

Latoya has a **great figure.**

Emily has **gorgeous hair.**

Dena dresses *beautifully.*

All I can see is a pimple on my face!

I always wanted to sing on Broadway.

I tried out for chorus and made it.

Now when I get up there to sing with
      a hundred other kids
      I worry that everyone
      is just looking at me.

I think I left my confidence back
in the elementary school.

I love to play ball but I hate gym.

Please don't ask me to undress.

    I'm skinny,

        I'm fat,

I'm tall,

      I'm small,

    I have thin hair,

      I have too much hair,

I don't even need a bra!

My English teacher asked me
To stay after class.

She said I write with great sensitivity
and I was cultured, humane, and very mature.

Thank heavens she didn't say that stuff
In front of the class!

I'm not good enough to make a varsity team.

But in this school we have "prep" teams.

We also have sports in which there is a no cut policy

It feels great to be a part of a team even
though I know I'm not a super star athlete.

We went on a field trip to Washington D.C.

We saw the Capitol building, the Smithsonian Museum, and the White House.

The best part of the trip was when we held hands all the way home on the bus.

I think we're going steady.

I don't care if the food is good or bad in the lunchroom.

All I care about is that ***it's the only place*** I can sit and talk with my friends.

Am I an adult or child?

I'm allowed to watch the house
    for a little while but never
    for a weekend.

At the movies
    I pay adult prices.

However, I'm not allowed to
    see R-rated films.

I ask again,
    Is a teenager an adult or child?

Go Team! Go Team! #1

Farewell **to** **Middle** School

I wanted to thank you,
visit you, write you
and show my appreciation
for helping me for the rest
of my life.

As years passed I realized
you'd know that I loved you.

I now can find my way because of you.

But, I'll always remember my favorite teacher.

Everyone Does!!

One of the senior boys from our high school died in a car crash.

The older kids were very upset.

The high school called in grief counselors.

An odd thing happened.

About 50 of the juniors and seniors from the high school came back to the middle school to talk to our teachers.

That's why I'll miss the middle school.

Our teachers always take the time to discuss our problems.

They always seem to have time for us.

For many of us, the middle school is our home away from home.

We had a moving-up dance *when we graduated* from the middle school.

In the gym, the teachers' pasted hearts on the wall with a **personal poem** written about *every student in the graduating class.*

I wonder if the high school teachers will care about us in the same way?

You taught me *how to sail,*
　　through space upon a comet's tail.

You taught me *how to fly,*
　　to sail the skies on wings untried.

You taught me *how to soar,*
　　to see things never seen before.

But most importantly of all,
　　You taught me *how to fall!*

You taught me *how to cry,*
　　to release feelings deep inside.

You taught me *how to laugh,*
　　and travel off the beaten path.

You taught me *how to dream,*
　　to face the future sight-unseen.

You taught me *how to be,*
　　the only thing I can be,
　　me.

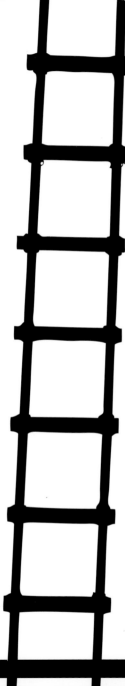

About the Author

Robert Ricken served as principal and superintendent in the Mineola School District for 22 years, and has also served six other districts as an interim superintendent. He is presently teaching educational administration at Long Island University, C.W. Post Campus.

He is the author of many books and has also written extensively for news magazines and newspapers. Dr. Ricken has presented well over 100 workshops and has been the keynote speaker for several national education associations.

Awards given to him include the Administrator of the Year by Phi Delta Kappa, Hofstra University Administrator of the Year, given by the Nassau-Suffolk Educator's Association. He received the Martin Luther King Jr. Recognition Award by Nassau County for his efforts to reduce prejudice in schools and the community. Recently he was presented with New York State Middle School Association's Ross Burkhardt Award for his outstanding contribution to middle level education.